Let's Draw

DiNoSaurs

by MANNY and ROCHELLE VALDIVIA

Copyright © 2000 McClanahan Book Company, Inc.
All rights reserved.
Published by McClanahan Book Company, Inc.
23 West 26th Street, New York, NY 10010
Printed in the U.S.A.
ISBN: 0-7681-0221-9

10 9 8 7 6 5 4 3 2 1

TRICERATOPS

(try-SER-ah-tops)

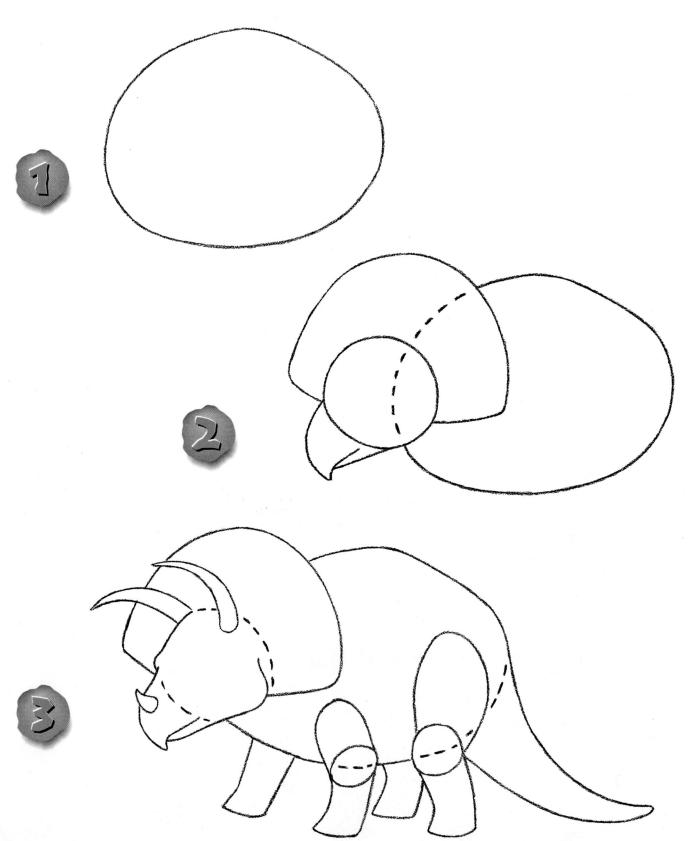

ANKYLOSAURUS
(An-KY-loh-SORE-us)

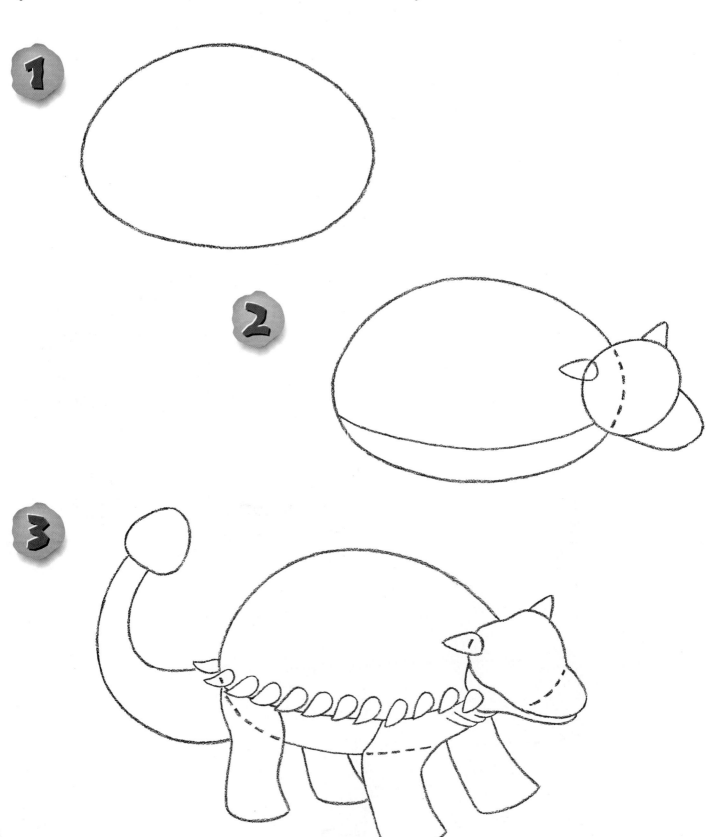

4

5

STEGOSAURUS
(STEG-oh-SORE-us)

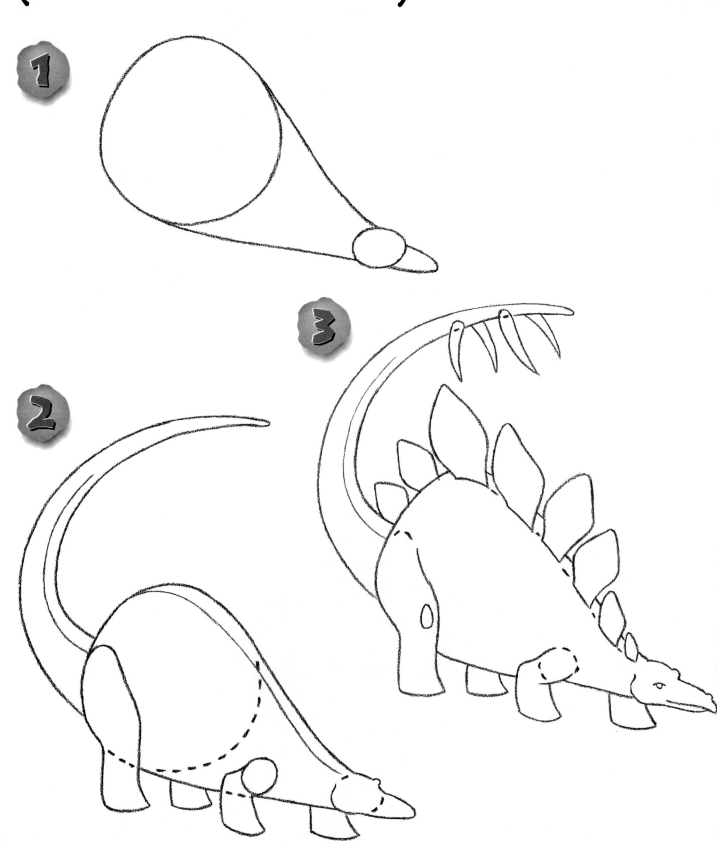

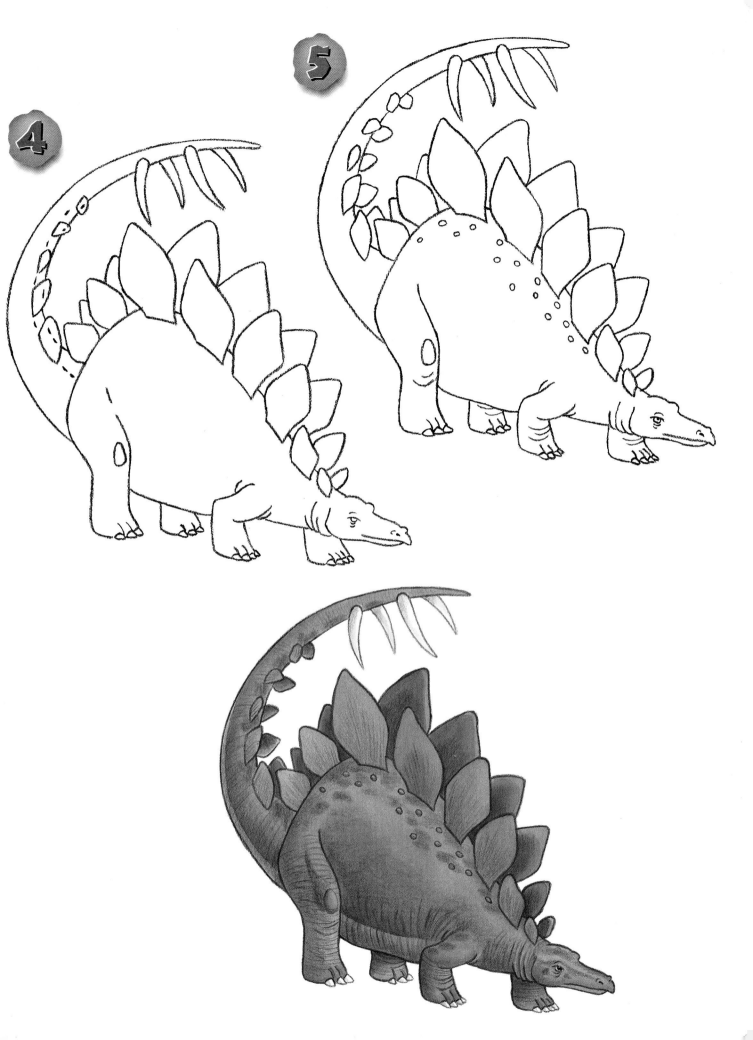

PARASAUROLOPHUS

(pair-ah-SORE-oh-LOH-fus)

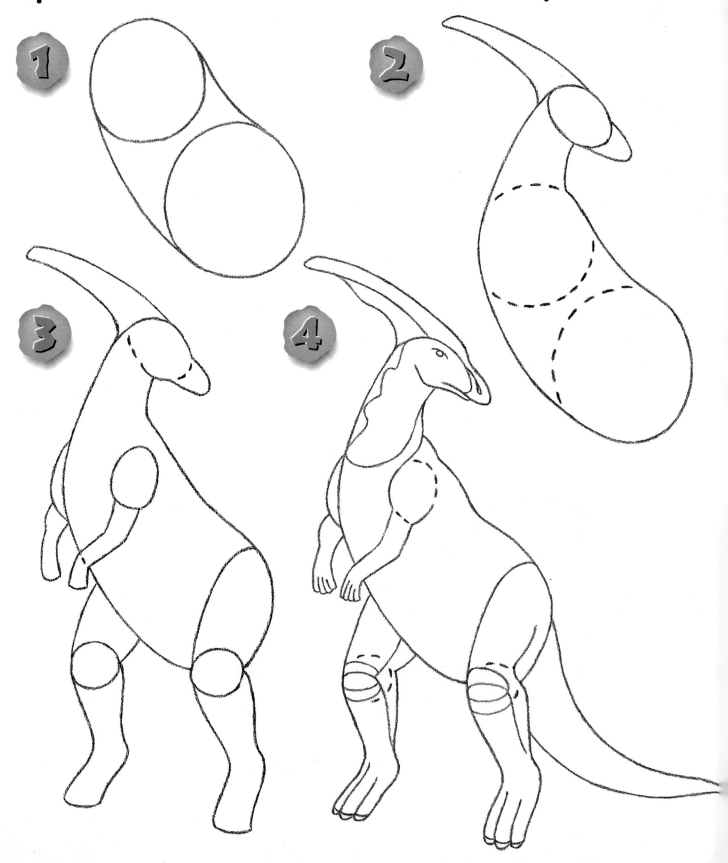

OVIRAPTOR
(OH-vih-RAP-tor)

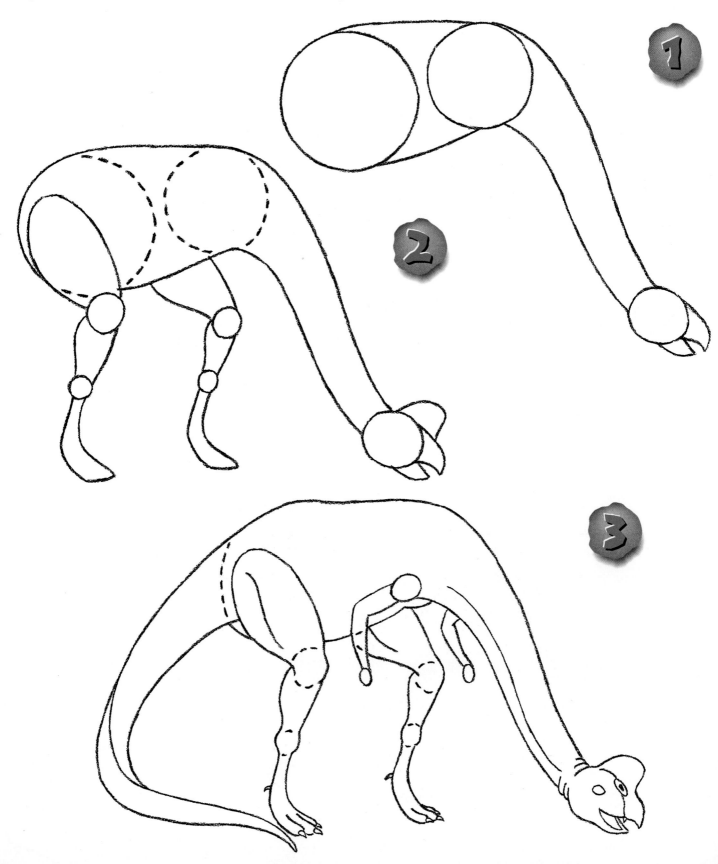

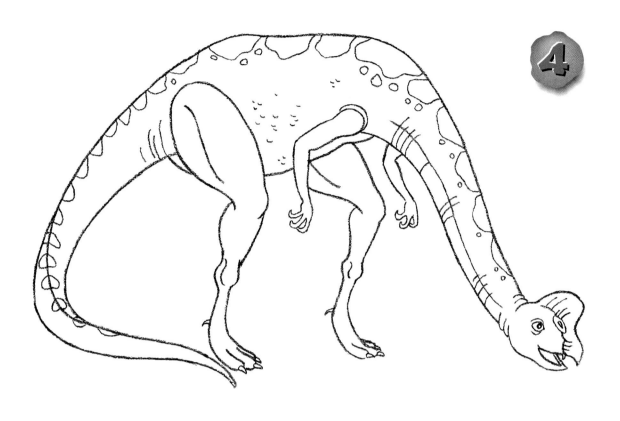

4

BRACHIOSAURUS

(BRAK-ee-oh-SORE-us)

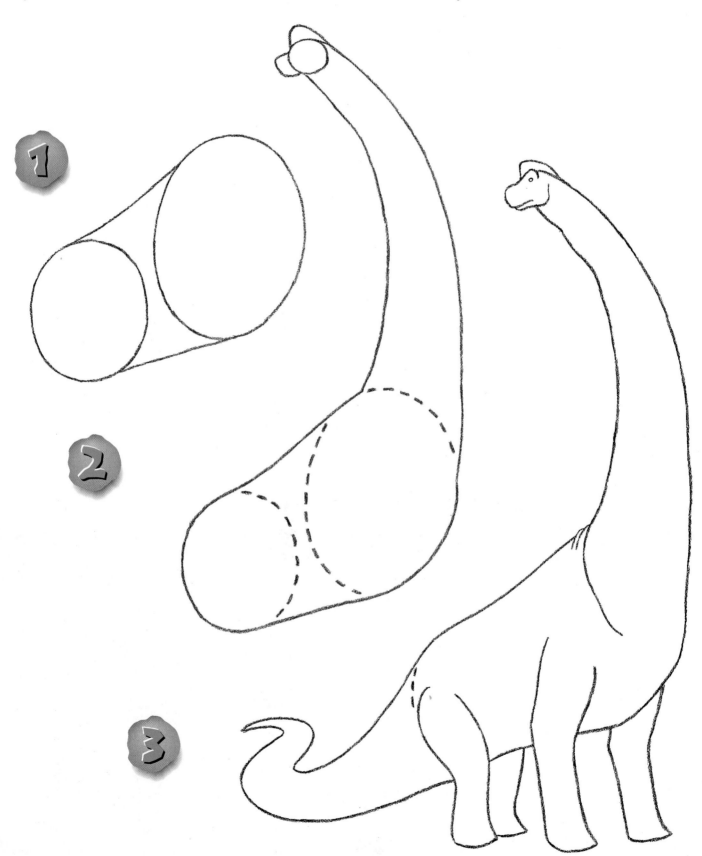

COELOPHYSIS

(SEE-loh-FY-sis)

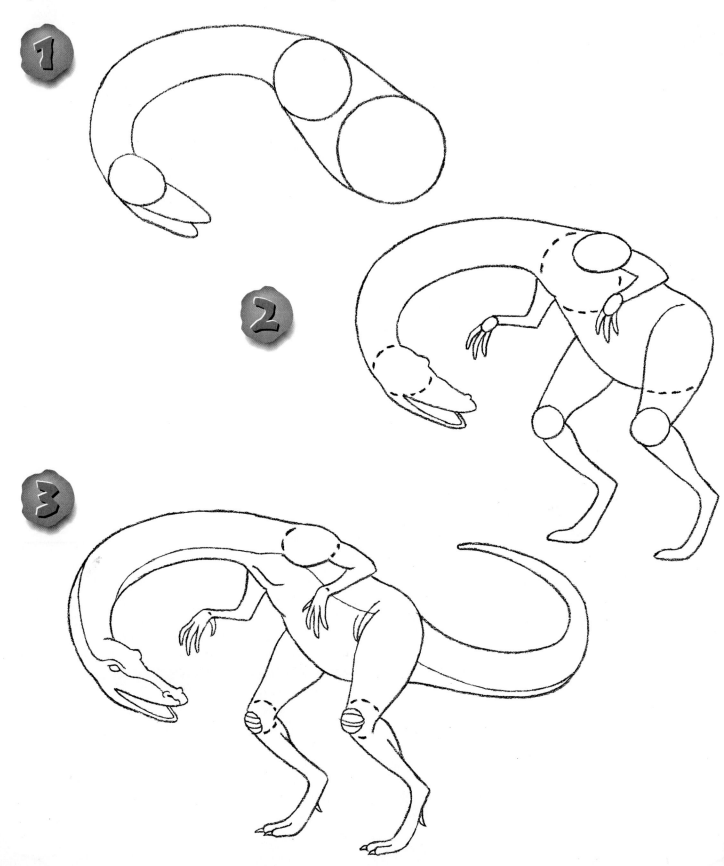

PACHYCEPHALOSAURUS
(PAK-ee-SEF-ah-loh-SORE-us)

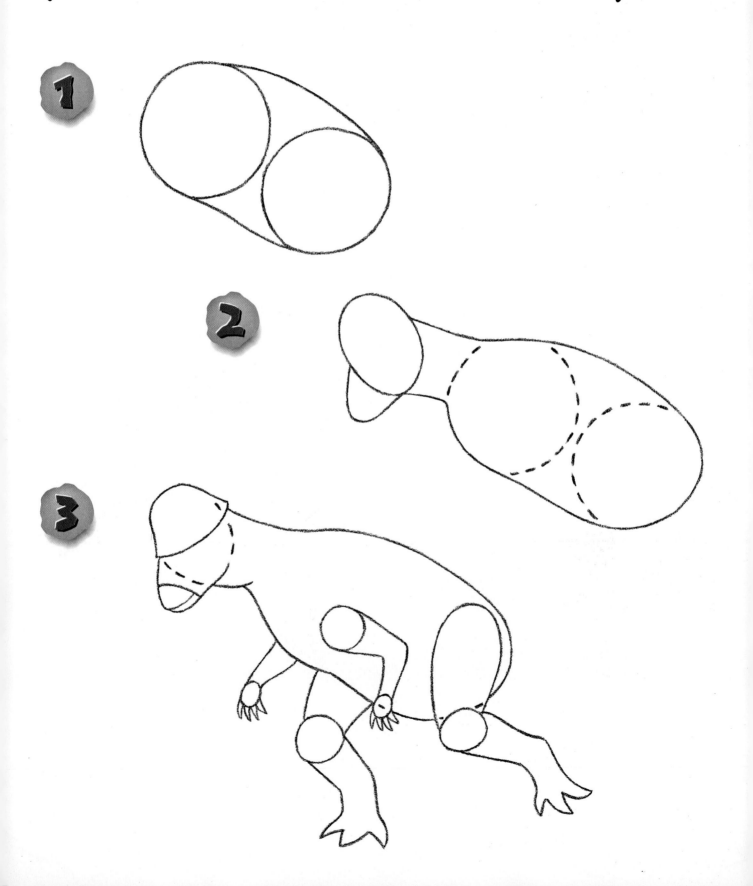

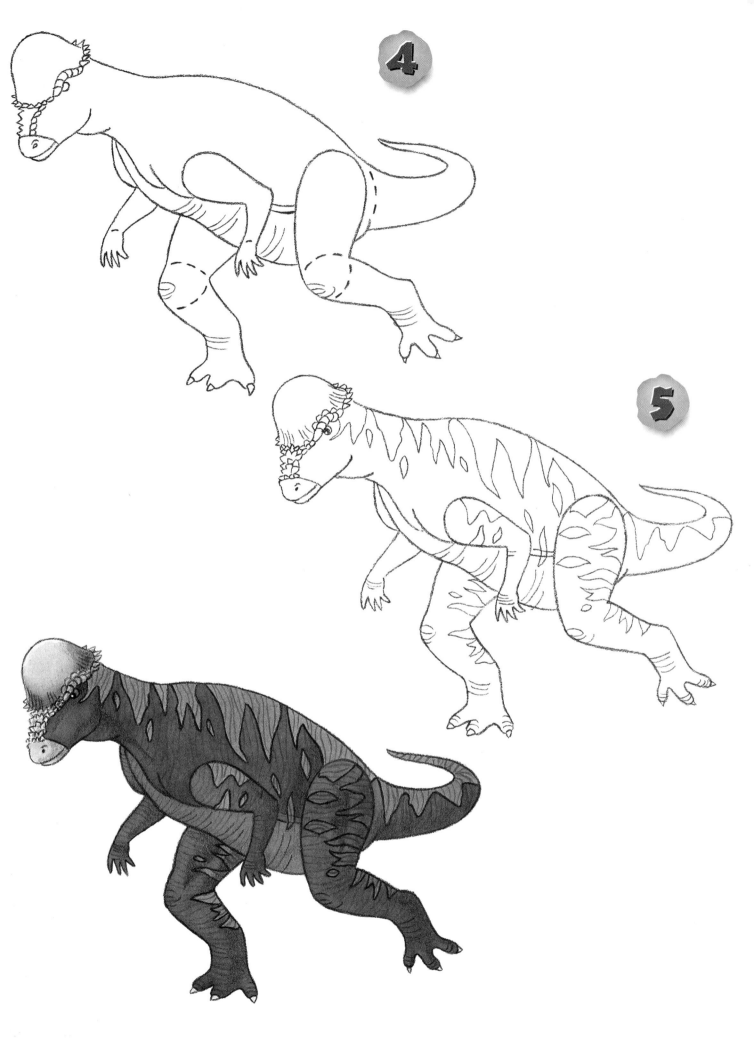

STRUTHIOMIMUS
(STRU-thee-oh-MY-mus)

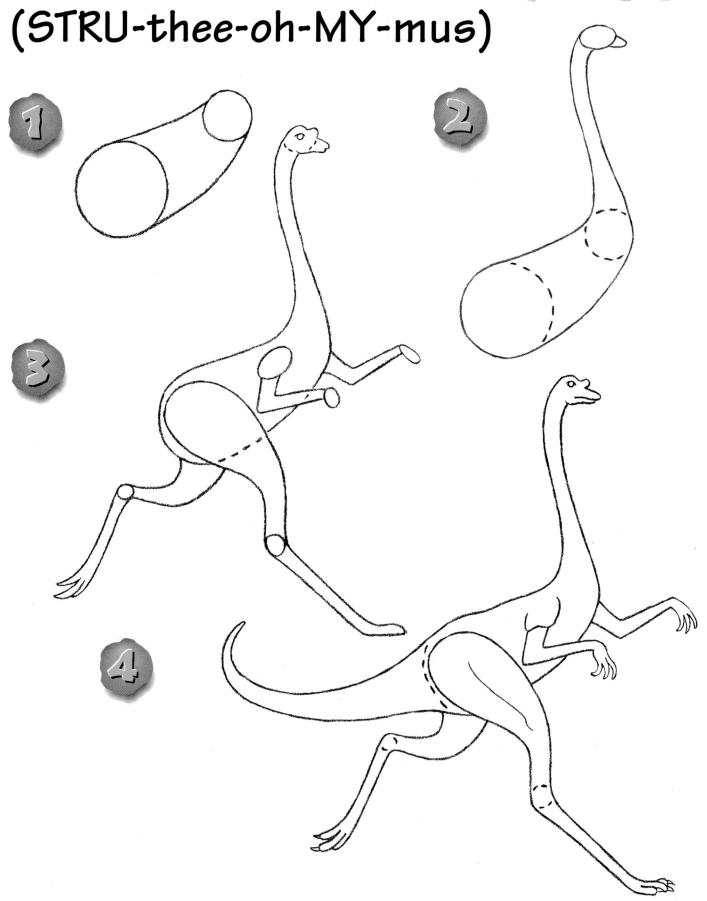

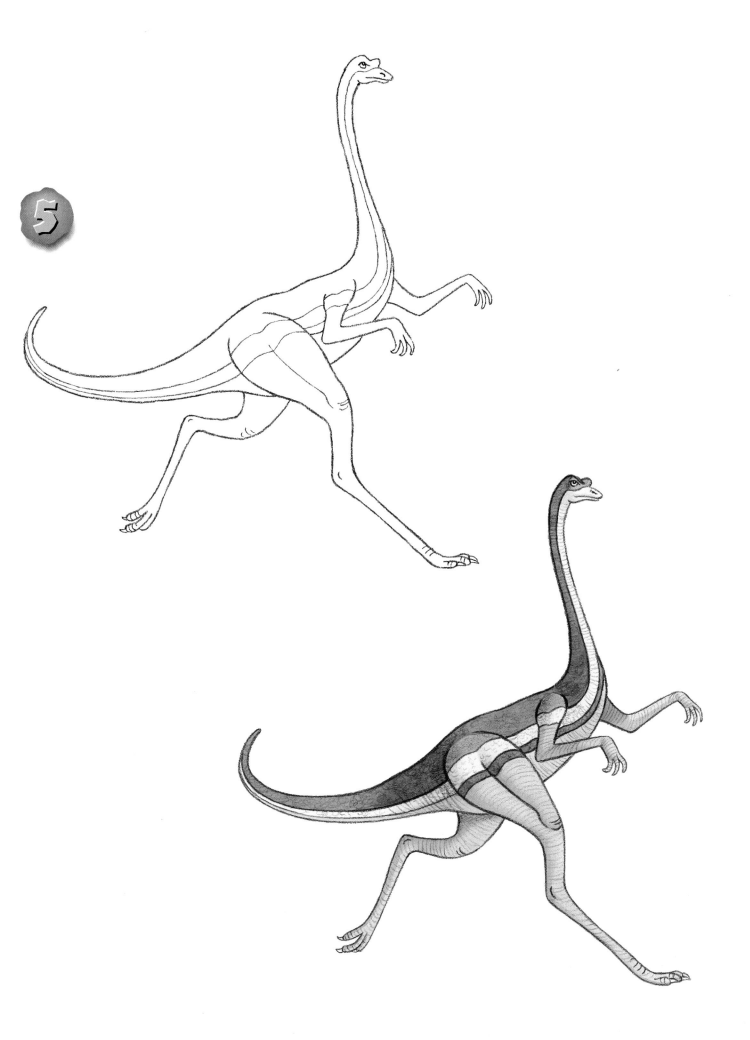

SPINOSAURUS
(SPY-no-SORE-us)

1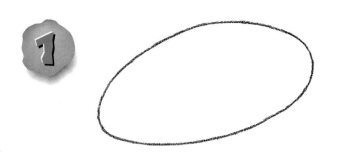

2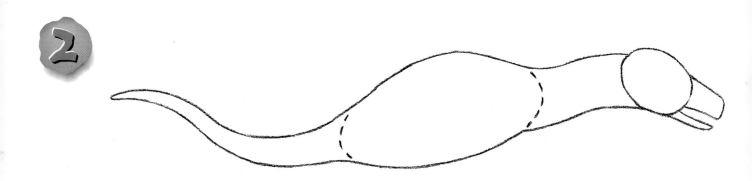

3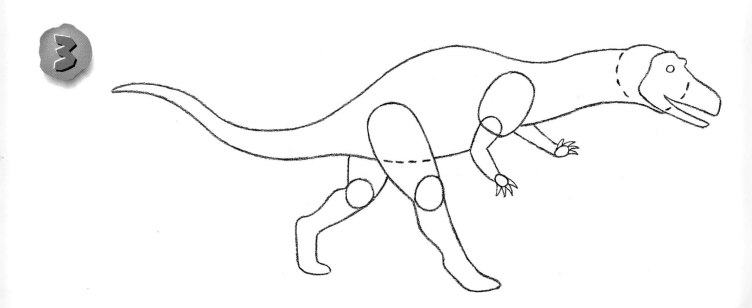

PLESIOSAURUS
(PLEE-see-oh-SORE-us)

APATOSAURUS
(a-PAT-oh-SORE-us)

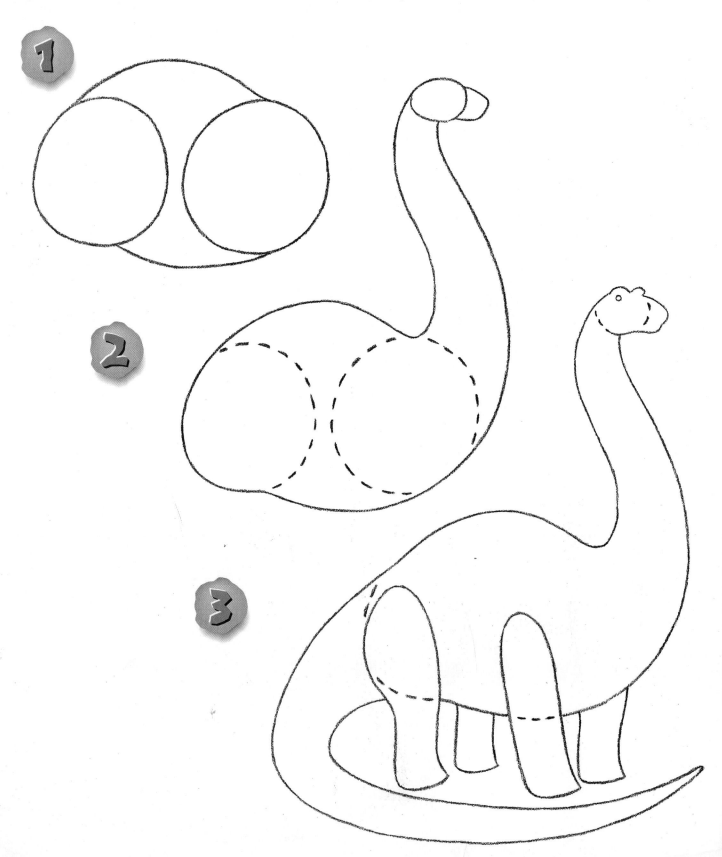

PTERANODON
(ter-RAN-oh-don)

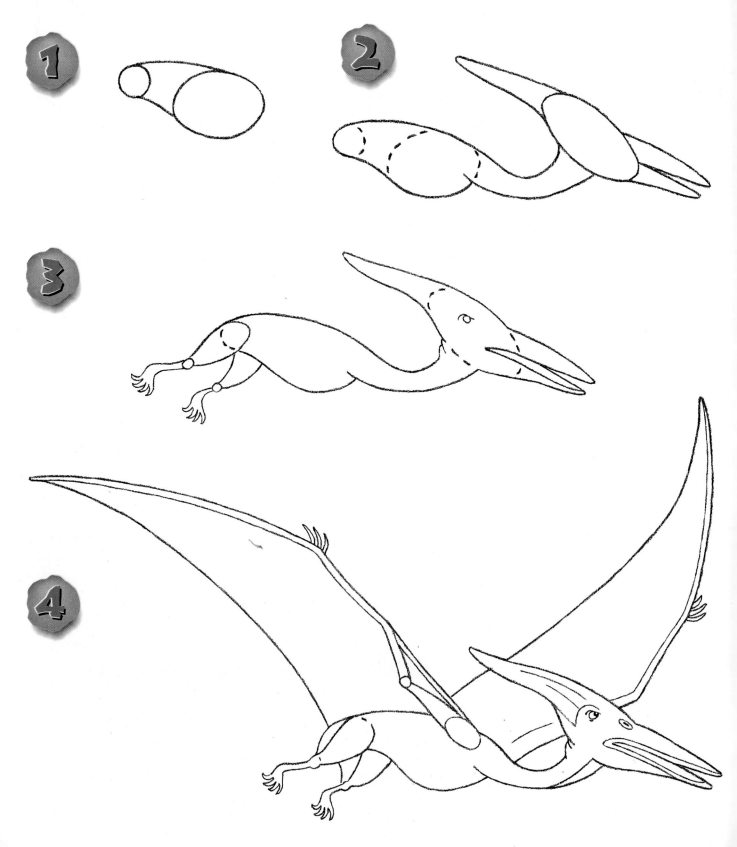

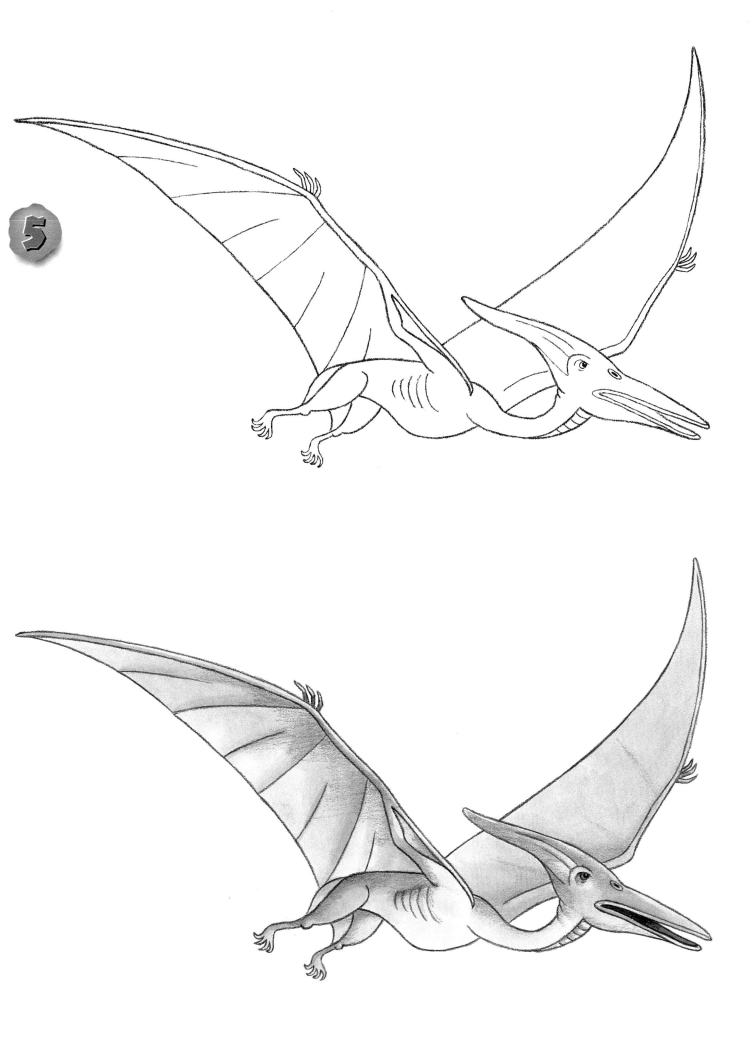

VELOCIRAPTOR
(VEL-oh-sih-RAP-tor)

TYRANNOSAURUS
(ty-RAN-oh-SORE-us)

LONG GONE

AUBREY SCHOOL
1075 Stratford Avenue
Burnaby, B. C.
V5B 3X9